D1508777

the Big Squeeze

Hugs & Inspirations
For Every Grown-Up Who Loves Teddy Bears

Susan Mangiero

This publication (in all formats) is published by Happy Day Press,
an imprint owned by I Paint With Words, LLC.

Copyright © 2017 by Susan Mangiero. All rights reserved. No part of this publication may be reproduced, stored in a retrieval system, distributed or transmitted in any form or by any means, including photocopying, recording, or other electronic or mechanical methods, without the prior written permission of the publisher.

ISBN 978-0-9975023-2-9 (Hardcover)
ISBN 978-0-9975023-1-2 (Kindle)

This publication is available at special discounts when purchased in bulk for marketing and sales promotions as well as for fundraising or educational use. In addition, special editions or book excerpts can be created to a buyer's specification. For information, contact the Head of Sales at the address below or send an email to sales@hugsandjoy.com.

I Paint With Words, LLC
929 White Plains Road, Number 377
Trumbull, CT 06611
www.hugsandjoy.com

Printed in Canada
First Printing January 2017

Publisher's Note: Any general reference to research or events is based on publicly available information, is provided for educational purposes only and is not the result of any in-depth investigation. Interested persons should contact the source directly to independently verify details. This publication (in any form and any accompanying websites) is not designed to, and does not provide, financial, health and/or life planning advice. Neither Susan Mangiero nor I Paint With Words, LLC is liable or responsible for the use of the information provided in this publication (in any form) or as part of the accompanying website at www.hugsandjoy.com.

To my wonderful husband George—
my favorite "teddy bear" to hug

Contents

Introduction

Millions of us squeeze our teddy bears on a regular basis, whether they are new additions to our household or ones cherished since childhood. We are drawn to our furry friends because we know that there is something magical about cuddling a favorite plush pal. They require minimal upkeep, are loyal companions and ask only for hugs and respect. Whether you take them on a business trip (as surveys show adults do), tuck them under your arms when you sleep at night or clutch them tight after a bad day, teddy bears deliver what you need. They are always there for you.

I have long found solace and joy in the warmth of a teddy bear embrace. As current caretaker of nearly fifty "best buds," I know firsthand the power of hugs. I've squeezed many a teddy to help with life challenges and relish the chance to pay it forward as often as I can. A teddy bear is a wonderful gift to give and receive. It's a way to give the recipient permission to be playful and childlike again. That's not all. A teddy bear can make it easier to acknowledge feelings such as loneliness or sadness.

As lovable as they are, teddy bears are more than just snug worthy. Various scientific studies explain how hugging teddy bears can help to boost self-esteem, reduce stress and encourage wellbeing. It's no surprise then that teddy bears show up in hospitals or find their way to those in need of cuddles.

As we know, communities can, and often, hurt too. That's why it's not at all uncommon to share the desire for a better world by donating teddy bears to those who have suffered tragedy or simply to show empathy and support. Kindness is a language that everyone understands, whether young or old, rich or poor, healthy or ill. What better ambassador is there than a huggable teddy bear? It's unsurprising that teddies are recognized with dedicated holidays such as National Hugging Day every January 21 and National Teddy Bear Day every September 9. The wonder of teddy bears is universal and enduring. Their presence is an integral part of the tapestry of events and people we call life. We rely on teddies to help us accept, celebrate, heal, love, try and share.

At a time when plenty of things seem beyond our control, squeezing a cushy teddy bear can be an easy way to self-care and focus squarely on the positive. It's hard to imagine a world without teddy bears and hugs that let us experience bliss, serenity and a connection to others. Motivated by gratitude for what is and hope for what can be, I wrote *The Big Squeeze* as an invitation to readers to indulge their teddy bear habit and take pleasure in the sweetness of welcome hugs and kind gestures. Most of all, this book is a celebration of the joy that teddy bears offer and the promise of everything that is good.

ACCEPT

that life has its **UPS** and **DOWNS**.

You might be **FEELING** less than tip top . . .

trying to mend a broken
HEART . . .

or missing
SOMEONE
SPECIAL
or in need of
making a
new pal.

Often it **DOESN'T MATTER** what has you down . . .

you just want
COMFORT . . .

NURTURING . . .

or reassurance
and **CALM**.

When life hands you lemons, **SQUEEZE HARD** and take a nap.

CELEBRATE

the **"WOW"**
in life
every chance
you get.

Have a
PARTY.

Bring out
the
BALLOONS.

Wear a **FUNNY HAT.**

SING OUT LOUD even if you can't carry a tune.

JUMP AROUND
just because
it feels good.

Make
it a
habit to
TREAT
yourself
often.

Schedule time to **PLAY** and **ENJOY** yourself.

LAUGH
like
nothing
else
matters.

HEAL

with a **FOCUS** on
what you need.

Pay attention to how you **FEEL**.

Know
when to
take it
EASY.

SURROUND
yourself
with those
who care.

Get lots
of **REST**.

PROTECT
yourself.

Be
SILLY.

Stay
STRONG.

Be open to the **WISDOM** of others.

Search for the **GOOD STUFF** each day offers.

Consider a new perspective when things seem **FUZZY**.

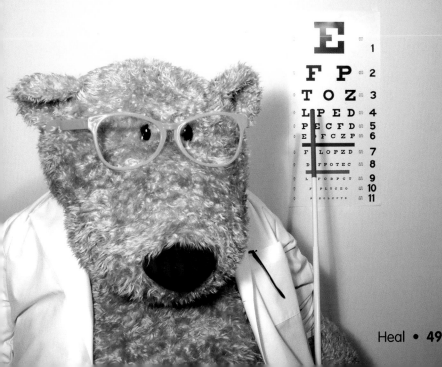

Give
yourself
permission
to
**QUIETLY
REFLECT**.

LOVE

is a little word
with a
BIG IMPACT.

It is a message that
BEARS
REPEATING.

Love
MULTIPLIES ...

CONNECTS . . .

and **EMBRACES** differences.

There is
ROMANCE . . .

love of **FAMILY** . . .

affection from
FRIENDS . . .

and warm
hellos from
NEIGHBORS.

Love **FREES** you
to be your true self . . .

and enhances what makes you **SPECIAL**.

Always keep love
in your heart from
MORNING . .

until
NIGHT.

TRY

even when
**GETTING
STARTED**
seems hard.

There is no shortage of things to **LEARN** . . .

ADVENTURES
to take . . .

EXPERIENCES
to savor . . .

and **POSSIBILITIES**
you never thought
of before.

Be your own
BEST FAN.

Keep the
door to
opportunity
**WIDE
OPEN**.

Regularly assess your **WORK-TO-FUN** ratio

Prudently
CONSIDER
the risks.

If it seems
right
for you,
**SPREAD
YOUR
WINGS**
and soar.

SHARE

the **MAGIC**
and the
MOMENT.

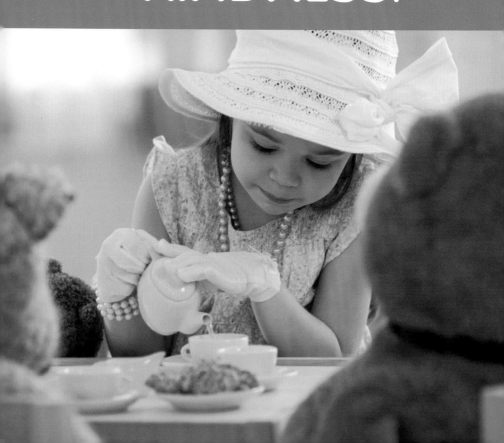

Feed the soul with **KINDNESS**.

Show up to **PROVIDE SUPPORT** . . .

even if
it's just to
LISTEN
and
EMPATHIZE.

Face
uncertainty
TOGETHER.

REMEMBER
the past.

CHERISH the extraordinary ordinary.

CUDDLE and **HUDDLE.**

EXERCISE your
hug muscles often.

Spread the
HAPPY...

and delight
in all that is
AMAZING.

Photography Credits

Fotalia: aireo pp. 23, 26; aldegonde le compte pp. 14–15;
alexsfoto pp. 62–63; Alfonso de Tomás p. 55; aliaj pp. 84–85; andreusk p. 72;
anna karwowska p. 45; AR Images p. 9; arthito p. 69; auryndrikson p. 12;
BillionPhotos.com pp. 28–29, 90; Blend Images pp. 34–35, 82, 88;
bluebat p. 32; bluejeanstock p. 60; bob p. 61; Brebca p. 39; bualuang_
fotalia pp. 4, 46; candy1812 p. 11; component p. 13; Cora Müller pp. 40–41;
D.R. p. 44; Deyan Georgiev pp. 50–51; evonnedale p. 89;
Garevskaya Elina p. 76; gugelleonid p. 17; hakase420 p. 83;
Jeanette Dietl p. 77; Jiri Hera p. 75; jozsitoeroe pp. 78–79; jstaley4011 p. 64;
karenfoleyphoto p. 49; katy_89 pp. 58–59; kazanovskyiphoto (Front Cover);
KittyKat pp. 24–25; Maruba p. 74; msharova p. 19; nokinka p. 54;
Ocskay Mark p. 87; PAO joke p. 18; Patryk Kosmider p. 57;
pavel siamionov p. 47; Phils Photography p. 16; Springfield Gallery p. 67;
suthisak p. 53; Tanja pp. 20–21; thaninee p. 65; tuanyick p. 27; villorejo p. 48;
volkovslava p. 81; vrstudio p. 66; waewkid p. 56; weseetheworld p. 70;
Westend61 pp 42–43; Zarya Maxim p. 33; zmijak pp. 30–31.

Getty Images: Dorling Kindersley pp. 92–93; Frank Gaglione p. 71.

iStock by Getty Images: dtimiraos p. 37; Fesus Robert Levente (Back Cover);
Halfpoint p. 86; ivanastar p. 91; MariyaL p. 73; XiXinXing p. 38.

Susan Mangiero p. 96.

Acknowledgments

Many thanks to the team of knowledgeable and experienced professionals who assisted me during the past twelve months as my idea for an inspirational book about kindness to others and ourselves became a publishing reality. Their individual contributions were invaluable and made the creative process rewarding and fun.

Desktop Miracles, Inc. CEO Barry Kerrigan was beyond generous in sharing his expert suggestions about book production, marketing and selling strategies. Del LeMond, Creative Director, did an amazing job with his design and typesetting of *The Big Squeeze*.

I am likewise deeply grateful to Susan Suffes with Your Book is My Business, Inc. for her cheerfulness, diligence in editing content and intuitive understanding about what readers like.

About the Author

SUSAN MANGIERO is an economist, writer and sometimes college professor. When not working on her award-winning business blog, teaching or analyzing numbers, you can find Susan shopping for new teddy bears to add to the family. Ever an optimist, she looks for the fun, quirky and inspiring things in life that bring people together.